After the Nuclear Accident - V.Babenko

AFTER THE NUCLEAR ACCIDENT
HOW TO PROTECT AGAINST RADIATION –
A PRACTICAL GUIDE

VLADIMIR BABENKO

(Photo page 39)

Translated and adapted from French (*Après l'accident Atomique*)
by Susanne Urban,
spokesperson for Nordic Network against Uraniumweapons
member of Womens International League for Peace and Freedom - Bergen,
Norway

"This is our earth, this is where we live!"

AFTER THE NUCLEAR ACCIDENT

HOW TO PROTECT AGAINST RADIATION – A PRACTICAL GUIDE

CONTENT

PREFACE FOR THE ENGLISH VERSION
FROM CHERNOBYL TO FUKUSHIMA

"Nuclear accidents have a starting point, but in reality these events have no end."[1] Whether we look at the major, publicized incidents—Chernobyl,[2] Three Mile Island,[3] Fukushima—or the "lesser-known" accidents—Windscale, Mayak,[4] Detroit,[5] among others—the consequences of these accidents have continued wreaking havoc long after the original problem has been contained. They have resulted, among other things, in the release of radioactivity into the environment, resulting in additional cancers, birth defects, and barriers to reproduction. Furthermore, radioactivity is routinely released from all industrial nuclear sites even during non-accident operations. And as a 1985 report by the United Nations Environment Programme concluded, "no level of exposure to radiation can be described as safe."[6]

---

[1] Mary Olsen, "United States," *Costs, risks, and myths of nuclear power*, Reaching Critical Will of the Women's International League for Peace and Freedom, 2011, p. 94.

[2] Chernobyl: see also the above link.

[3] The body of literature on Three Mile Island is large and diverse. As a starting place for information see
http://www.nirs.org/reactorwatch/accidents/accidentshome.htm.

[4] Wikipedia has fairly decent accounts of this event at
http://en.wikipedia.org/wiki/Kyshtym_disaster.

[5] One account of the Fermi-1 partial core melt is by John Fuller, "We Almost Lost Detroit," *Reader's Digest Press*, 1975.

[6] "Radiation—doses, effects, risks," United Nations Environment Program, December 1985.

In a 2011 study produced after the Fukushima catastrophe, Marguerite Finn of the UK Section of the Women's International League for Peace and Freedom (WILPF) examined the case of Sellafield in West Cumbria. Sellafield was originally called Windscale and was established to burn uranium and produce plutonium quickly for the UK's first nuclear bomb. In 1957, in an attempt to cut corners and increase the rate of plutonium production, some uranium cartridges overheated and a fire broke out in the reactor. "Personnel were unable to extinguish the fire for several days and a plume of radioactive contamination was released into the atmosphere, falling on cities in the north of England," she explained.

"Sellafield today is a vast, leaky nuclear complex," wrote Finn. "In 1994, a Thermal Oxide Reprocessing Plant (THORP) was opened at Sellafield to reprocess irradiated oxide nuclear fuel from both the UK and foreign reactors. In 2005, however, 83,000 litres of radioactive waste was found to have leaked from a cracked pipe in the Thorp plant into a huge stainless-steel container lined concrete chamber built to contain leaks. A discrepancy between the amount of material entering and exiting the Thorp processing system was first noticed in August 2004 but no action was taken at the time. It was not until ten months later in April 2005, that operators discovered the enormity of the leak, which amounted to some 19 tonnes of uranium and 160 kilograms of plutonium. Although no radiation was released into the environment, the event was given a Level 3 rating on the International Nuclear Event scale and

     After the Nuclear Accident – V.Babenko

Sizewell Ltd was fined £500,000 for breaching health and safety laws."[7]

This is but one accident of many that have occurred. Most recently, we have witnessed the devastation caused by the radioactive catastrophe in Japan. At 2:46 pm on 11 March 2011, a massive earthquake struck the northeast of Japan, causing a tsunami of immense devastation and leading to the disaster at the Fukushima Dai-ichi Nuclear Power Station. The loss of life, livelihoods, homes, and communities was catastrophic. And while the human spirit begins to rebuild from the natural disasters, piecing lives and homes back together, the effects of the nuclear disaster will go on for generations. Just as we learned of the details of the situation at Fukushima Dai-ichi only after the worst had happened, so too will the Japanese people and their neighbours only later discover the full effects of the radiation released from the meltdowns and explosions.

Radiation is long lasting and has inter-generational effects, as the survivors of Hiroshima and Nagasaki know only too well. In February 2011, a group of Hibakusha, atomic bomb survivors from Japan, asserted that radiation, whatever its source, is a major threat to humanity and the environment and called for phasing-out all sources of radiation—from uranium mining, nuclear reactors, nuclear accidents, nuclear weapons development and testing, and nuclear waste—and for investment in renewable, clean

---

[7] Marguerite Finn, "United Kingdom," *Costs, risks, and myths of nuclear power*, Reaching Critical Will of the Women's International League for Peace and Freedom, 2011, pp. 91–92.

energy for a sustainable future.[8] It is a terrible tragedy that the very country that sustained and survived an attack with nuclear weapons is today sustaining radiation exposure and contamination from nuclear power.[9]

The experience of Fukushima has been particularly frustrating for those living in the vicinity of the plant. WILPF Japan member Kozue Akibayashi explained in September 2011 that nobody in a responsible position had at that point "provided necessary information to the public about the status of the radiation leaks, anticipated impacts, or polices to ensure the safety of people." She described reports that "many residents in the surrounding areas of the Fukushima Dai-ichi plant had to make decisions about evacuation without sufficient information and headed to locations that were later revealed to have been contaminated with higher levels of radiation, because their assumption of the wind direction was incorrect…. Now many residents are struggling with very little help to figure out what safety measures they can take, especially to protect children who are more vulnerable to radiation."[10]

This practical guide provides information on living with radiation. It is extremely unfortunate that such information is neces-

---

[8]Global Hibakusha Forum Statement for a Nuclear-Free World, 5 February 2011, at
http://www.peaceboat.org/english/?page=view&nr=20&type=23&menu=62.

[9] *WILPF Statement on Japan's nuclear crisis, 15 March 2011, at http://www.wilpfinternational.org/statements/2011/Japan.html.*

[10] Kozue Akibayashi, "Preface," Costs, risks, and myths of nuclear power, Reaching Critical Will of the Women's International League for Peace and Freedom, 2011, p. 1.

sary. But with over 400 nuclear reactors operating throughout the world, it seems sensible for basic knowledge about radioactivity to be made available.

As Japanese novelist Haruki Murakami noted in a June 2011 prize-acceptance speech in Barcelona, "Nuclear power plants, which were supposed to be efficient, instead offer us a vision of hell."[11]

Ray Acheson 19.06.2013

Ray Acheson is the programme director of Reaching Critical Will, the disarmament programme of the Women's International League for Peace and Freedom, based in New York.

---

[11] Haruki Murakami, "As an Unrealistic Dreamer," speech for the Catalunya International Prize, 10 June 2011, at *http://www.senrinomichi.com/?p=2728.*

After the Nuclear Accident – V.Babenko

FIRST PART: INFORMING YOURSELF

RADIOACTIVITY

Matter is composed of atoms that are joined in chemical combinations called molecules. Each atom consists of a nucleus, which is composed of smaller elementary particles called protons and neutrons; around this nucleus orbit the same number of electrons as there are protons in the nucleus. The number of protons in the nucleus is called the atomic number and determines the type of atom. There are 98 naturally occurring types of atoms or chemical elements. Protons are positively charged, neutrons have no charge and electrons are negatively charged; normally an atom possesses the same number of protons as electrons, the charges balance each other. If an atom gains or loses electrons it becomes charged and is called an ion. Radioactivity is a characteristic of some atomic nuclei where they transform themselves spontaneously, falling apart to form distinct new atomic nuclei.

The same atomic element can occur in both radioactive and stable variations: the only difference being the number of neutrons in the nucleus. Isotopes are atoms with the same number of protons (therefore the same chemical element) but different numbers of neutrons. Radioactive isotopes are called radionuclides.

For example the nucleus in the simplest of elements, hydrogen, contains only one proton and no neutron; other elements have several protons and may have, in addition, a variable number of neutrons. Hydrogen for example, has two additional isotopes, deuterium (that is stable, with one proton and one neutron), and tritium (that is radioactive, with one proton and two neutrons).

The disintegration of a nucleus is often associated with emission of high-energy particles and radiation with different energies that hit all matter that they meet on their way, for instance cells in the human body.

These emissions have sufficient energy to disrupt molecular bonds and remove electrons from the atoms that form a molecule. They are referred to as "ionizing radiation". We distinguish between different types of ionizing radiation: alpha (α)-particle emission that emits a helium nucleus, beta (β)-particle emission where the nucleus emits an electron and gamma (γ)-photon emission, in which the nucleus emits a type of electromagnetic radiation similar to x-rays, but with greater energy (see fact box).

The different types of radiation

We commonly distinguish between different radioactive transformations depending on the particle type that is released during disintegration of the atomic nucleus:

• **α-alpha radiation/** decay = emission of α-particles, i.e. helium nuclei

• **β-radiation** = emission of an electron

• **γ-radiation**, which is a type of electromagnetic radiation. The γ-rays do not correspond to a radioactive transformation of substance; it's the case of an electromagnetic radiation emanating from radioactive nuclei that are still active right after an α or β-decay.

The new nucleus is left with a surplus of energy. To get rid of this excess energy, the nucleus emits one or more γ-radiation doses with an energy output specific to this nucleus. The gamma ray configuration is characteristic of the atoms in a particular element - in a sense it is the signature of this radioactive element.

The energy carried by ionizing radiation allows it to penetrate and disrupt matter. The penetration ability depends on the radiation type and the matter's ability to stop the radiation. This defines the different material thicknesses required to shield us from ionizing radiation.

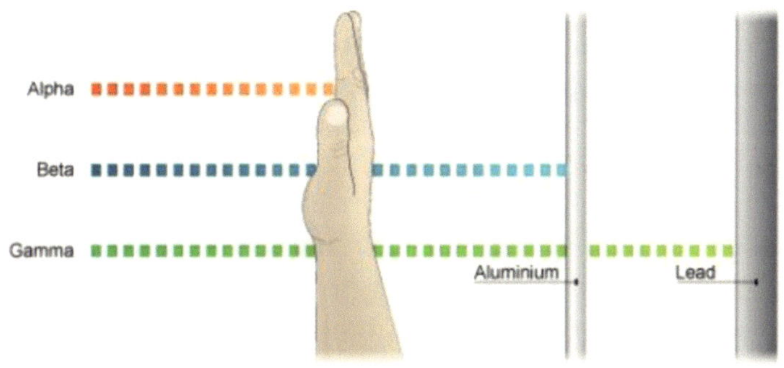

The most common radioactive transformation is β-radiation or β-decay. It is characteristic of 45% of all known radionuclides. About 15% of radioactive nuclei disintegrate by emitting α-radiation. Such disintegration is characteristic of the heavier isotopes of the last elements in the periodic table and of some substances in the middle of the periodic table. α-rays cannot be produced by the light elements.

Radionuclides disintegrate into other radionuclides, which in turn disintegrate into new radionuclides. This chain of reactions ends when the disintegration products are non-radioactive isotopes with stable nuclei.

Each radionuclide is characterized by the time it takes for half of a given mass to disintegrate naturally. This time is called the half-life of a radionuclide. Half-life can be a small fraction of a second to several billions of years, depending on the element.

Half-life of a radioactive material

The radioactive half-life for a given radioisotope is the time required for half of the atoms in a given mass of that isotope to "decay" or "disintegrate" naturally. In the case of a single atom the half-life is a statistical feature: it is the time in which the nucleus has a 50% probability of decay. This property is independent of the physical state (solid, liquid, gas) and of the surrounding conditions - such as temperature, pressure or electronic field; it only depends on the individual isotope. Consequently the number of original atoms decreases exponentially.

Radioactive half-life should not be confused with biological period, which is the time any amount of a radioactive isotope remains in the body before being excreted.

The half-life can vary from one radioactive isotope to another - from a fraction of a second to billions of years. Activity is inversely proportional to the isotope's half-life, that is, long half-life implies weak radiation.

The activity or rate of disintegration of a radionuclide is measured using the SI unit becquerel, abbreviated as Bq, which corresponds to one disintegration per second. (The old unit curie,

Ci, corresponds to the radioactivity in one gram of radium, $3,7x10^{10}$ Bq).

The energy carried by radiation (alpha, beta, gamma) following disintegration is measured in electron volts, eV, but usually with the multipliers keV (kilo-electron-volts or 1000 eV) or MeV, (mega electron volts or 1 000 000 eV). Chemical reactions usually involve just a few eV.

After Chernobyl[12] a large number of radionuclides fell on Belarusian soil. Some with short half-lives have already disintegrated, while others continue to radiate, bombarding anything that gets in their way with particles. See the following fact box.

---

[12] 26 April 1986, the world's worst nuclear accident (until then) happened in Chernobyl, Ukraine, 100 km north of Kiev. An explosive fire devastated reactor 4, a water-cooled graphite reactor. A total of 800,000 people participated in fighting the fire and securing the site. Risking life and health these "liquidators" engaged in a cleanup that prevented Europe from becoming uninhabitable. A zone of 30 km around the plant was declared danger zone, over 135,000 people were evacuated, but 10 years later still over 270,000 people lived in radioactive contaminated, restricted areas. A reinforced concrete sarcophagus was constructed over the reactor, but this shelter was later reported to be in poor condition. A new security shell, "New Safe Confinement", which is to be pushed over the reactor, is still under construction by June 2013. The curved metal shell will weigh 30,000 tons and last for "at least" 100 years. There have been funding problems, but the project will hopefully be completed in 2015.
Due to wind directions, radioactive fallout reached Britain, more then 2,000 km away. Radioactive particles became locked in upland peat and accumulated in grazing sheep. Controls where placed on 9,800 UK farms - for 14 years in Northern Ireland and 24 years in Scotland. In June 2012, after 26 years, restrictions have finally been lifted from all farms in Cumbria and Wales.

The major radioisotopes in the fallout from the Chernobyl nuclear power station

Isotope		Half-life	
Krypton-85 m	85mKr	4.4	hours
Neptunium-239	^{239}Np	2.35	days
Molybdenium-99	^{99}Mo	2.75	days
Tellurium-132	^{132}Te	3.26	days
Xenon-133	^{133}Xe	5.25	days
Iod-131	^{131}I	8.02	days
Barium-140	^{140}Ba	12.7	days
Cerium-141	^{141}Ce	32.2	days
Ruthenium-103	^{103}Ru	39.3	days
Strontium-89	^{89}Sr	50.6	days
Zirconium-95	^{95}Zr	64.0	days
Curium-242	^{242}Cu	163	days
Cerium-144	^{144}Ce	284	days
Ruthenium-106	^{106}Ru	368	days
Cesium-134	^{134}Cs	2.06	years
Krypton-85 m	^{85m}Kr	10.7	years
Plutonium-241	^{241}Pu	14.4	years
Strontium-90	^{90}Sr	29.12	years
Cesium-137	^{137}Cs	30	years
Plutonium-238	^{238}Pu	87.74	years
Plutonium-240	^{240}Pu	6537	years
Plutonium-239	^{239}Pu	24390	years

The population in the areas that were contaminated by radioactive fallout still receives radiation emitted by these nuclides. However, it is not the fairly weak radiation from radionuclides in the external environment, which poses the greatest health threat to residents.

> **The most serious consequences of radioactive pollution are radioactive particles entering the human body and getting bound to certain places there.**

Internal contamination by radionuclides is a source of internal radiation which persists as long as the radionuclide remains in the body, i.e. as long as they have not disintegrated or been removed.

What is the half-life of Strontium-90 and cesium-134, the most prevalent of long-term polluters in areas around Chernobyl? (See the previous table) The half-life for both strontium-90 (emitting exclusively β-radiation at 546 keV) and cesium-137 (emitting β-radiation at 514 keV, and γ-radiation at 662 keV) is about thirty years. In cases of radioactive-contamination similar to Chernobyl, one estimates that the concentration of radionuclides becomes negligible after about 10 half-lives. This **means:**

> **… it will take almost 300 years before the cesium and strontium that pollute the soil will no longer represent a problem of radioprotection.** It means that we ourselves, our children, our grandchildren, our great grandchildren - must learn to live in a radioactive environment. We must know how to reduce the effects of radiation on the organism to a minimum so that our children and grandchildren remain as healthy as possible.

Being subject to the effects of radiation, we must learn to live in polluted conditions.

POLLUTION FROM A SOURCE INSIDE THE BODY

Internal radiation is especially dangerous, since it affects the cells inside the human body directly. Of all the isotopes that were found in the fallout from the Chernobyl disaster, iodine, strontium and cesium are most widespread and most dangerous over both the short and the long term.

I-131: Iodine-131 emits β- and γ-radiation with a half-life of 8.07 days (and an activity of 4.6×10^{15} Bq/g) The disintegration-energy is at 960 keV, 606 keV from β- and 364 keV from gamma-radiation. The body easily absorbs iodine-131, concentrating it in the thyroid gland. Iodine-131 represents a real danger for a few months, after that it is as good as gone.

Cs-134: Cesium-134 has a half-life of 2.06 years. During a nuclear incident its percentage of radioactivity is equal to that of Cs-137, but since it disintegrates so much faster, its relative share is almost 0 after 20 years. It decays by emitting β-radiation at 2.05 MeV.

Cs-137: Cesium-137 emits β-and γ-radiation with a half-life of 30 years and an activity of 3.2×10^{12} Bq/g) The disintegration-energy is 1.176MeV, with 514 keV from β-, and 622 from γ-radiation. It is dangerous because of its strong radiation and long life. Cesium is an alkaline metal and is chemically similar to potassium. It spreads to the whole body. The biological half-life for it to be washed out of the organism is dependent on a person's age, varying from 15 to 150 days.

Sr-89 and Sr-90: Strontium-90 only emits β-radiation with energy of 546 keV; its half-life is 28.8 years (with an activity of 5.1 x

10^{12} Bq/g). Strontium-89 emits β-radiation with 1.463 MeV and with 52-day half-life and activity of 1.1 x 10^{15} Bq/g / 28,200 Ci / g). Strontium 89 is dangerous for a few years after an accident, while Strontium 90 can continue to be dangerous over several hundred years. Beyond emitting β-radiation, Strontium-90 atoms decay into yttrium-90, also radioactive, with a half-life of 64.2 hours, which falls apart by emitting β-particles with 2.27 MeV. Strontium is chemically similar to calcium and binds to bones and above all to the bone marrow, [where red blood cells are generated].

PATHWAYS TO INTERNAL CONTAMINATION

The population of the contaminated areas of Belarus is not only exposed to radiation from the environment, but are first and foremost subject to contamination by radioactive particles contained in locally produced food. Local foods are heavily contaminated by the radionuclides cesium-137 and strontium-90. Although the radiation doses are too weak to be detected by conventional detectors, this internal radiation is responsible for 70-90% of the total radiation burden their bodies are exposed to, that is, from both internal and external sources combined. Industrially manufactured products account for a small portion of the total load. Vegetables from private gardens or forest products such as wild game, fish from rivers and lakes, berries, mushrooms and medicinal herbs are a much more significant source. The explanation is that in Belarus the food industry is controlled, not only in terms of the manufactured products it supplies to the consumer, but also the raw materials to be processed are checked for radiation levels.

Cesium is water-soluble and spreads very quickly in the environment. One can readily find it at very large distances from the nuclear reactor in Chernobyl. When cesium enters the soil it's easily absorbed by vegetation. It is primarily through the food chain that radionuclides enter the human body, but it also occurs (to a much lesser extent) through inhalation (breathing) and by direct contact with the skin and mucous membranes.

Once they fell on Belarusian territory, the long-lived radionuclides were mostly deposited in the upper soil layer. Today the soil is the main source of radiation contamination in agricultural production.

Tree roots, especially from fruit trees, penetrate deeply into the ground and their fruit can be free from radioactivity, even in contaminated areas. The relationship between the amount of radionuclides in the soil and the amount absorbed by plants depends on soil type and plant breeds. The ratio is smallest for plants growing on fertile soil like "black earth" which only absorbs few nuclides. It is highest in the bog, peat soil, sandy soil and leached, poor soil, which absorbs most radiation. Lichens, mosses, mushrooms, legumes and grasses accumulate much. The presence of radionuclides in wild berries, that grow in contaminated areas, such as blueberries, cranberries and cloudberries, is also very high.

Radionuclides accumulate in different organs, entering the human body through various food chains:

VEGETABLE → HUMAN

PLANT → LIVESTOCK → MILK→ HUMAN

PLANT → ANIMAL → MEAT→ HUMAN

ALGAE → FISH→ HUMAN

A food chain can be extremely complex. If we separate milk and whey and the whey from contaminated cows is fed to calves, we get the following chain:

PLANT → LIVESTOCK → MILK → WHEY → ANIMAL → MEAT→ HUMAN

Here another quite complex and long food chain:
FOREST → FIREWOOD → FURNACE → ASHES → VEGE-TABLE GARDEN → VEGETABLES → HUMANS

These examples show us that it is possible to avoid the uptake of radionuclides in the human organism by using certain knowledge and daily habits, which we will now present.

The highest level of radiation contamination in milk ever measured by Belrad Institute was in milk from the Braguine district. The measured value was 5545 Bq/ l (becquerel per liter), at a time when the upper limit was set to 111 Bq/l. Eventually the reason was detected: two residents of Braguine district had collected hay in the 30-kilometer zone around the nuclear plant and had mixed the contaminated hay with hay from other areas. Cows cannot detect radiation in hay. Children drank the milk full of Cs-137, not having any ability to sense radiation either. The damage inflicted on the children by radiation was hundreds of times greater than any benefit they could have had from the milk itself.

(See illustration on contamination p. 44)

Another example: The largest concentration of radionuclides in a child's body was measured in 1999 in Narovlia-district, it was over 7,000 Bq/ kg. This family ate much wild game from the local forests. Wild boars know nothing about borders nor about the boundary of the forbidden zone around the nuclear plant. They live where they can find food. And they eat what they find in the woods. Boars from Narovlia have no more ability to detect radiation than the cows from Braguine - they eat what nature offers. The very short food chain: GAME → MAN had caused this strong accumulation of radionuclides in the two school girls from Narovlia.

**Food is the main source of radionuclides
in the human organism.**

A follow-up of the children in a village from Tchetchersk district focused on a large family where both children and parents had accumulated radiation levels that were ten to fifteen times higher than the acceptable limit. Radiation monitoring of foods they usually ate showed that their jam (from blueberries, cranberries and lingonberries) as well as salted mushrooms, were highly contaminated by cesium-137 and were unfit for human consumption. It is easy to understand the despair of this mother of five children: she had done a great amount of work picking and preserving berries and mushrooms, and she had spent some money on sugar, in the belief that she would have supplies for the children. Suddenly she hears that she must dispose of all that food. But she found the strength to do it. The members of this family were treated with an adsorbent based on apple pectin in order to excrete radionuclides from their bodies. The children had to do without mushrooms and blueberries picked in a forest with a radioactive environment of over 900 microroentgen/hr (the average radioactivity in the environment in an uncontaminated region is 5 microroentgen/hr). Finally, measurements taken in September 2002 showed that the specific radioactivity of cesium-137 had fallen to 40 Bq/ kg for the children and 70 Bq/ kg for the parents.

Let us again examine the food chains whereby radionuclides enter the human body: you see that it is enough to cut out a single link to restrict the amount of radionuclides entering the body or to add a link. If we for instance add "separation of milk" to the chain "VEGETABLE → LIVESTOCK → MILK → HUMAN ", the amount of radionuclides that will enter the human body will be limited because the majority of the radioactive particles will remain dissolved in the whey. Notice though, that this whey is unfit for consumption. If we remove mushrooms in a food chain, there will be less radionuclides to reach our bodies. If we add the link "SOAK-ING" between MUSHROOMS and HUMAN, radionuclides dissolved in water will not be able to contaminate the body.

THE IMPACT OF RADIATION ON HUMAN HEALTH

Nuclear energy, which is produced by radioactive decay can benefit man. But it causes terrible harm if it gets out of control. Medical studies conducted in recent years show that the Chernobyl disaster has had and still has an ongoing harmful effect on the people of Belarus. The average life span in Belarus today is shorter than in the neighbouring countries: Russia, Ukraine, Poland, Lithuania and Latvia. When asked about the cause of this, most of the people of Belarus blame Chernobyl.

Studies show that:
• The proportion of children in good health, which was at 85% before the disaster, has fallen to 20%
• Chronic diseases have increased from 10% to 20%
• All types of disease have increased
• The frequency of malformations in areas contaminated by Chernobyl are 2.3 times higher than countries average.

Two million people are suffering the consequences of the Chernobyl disaster, including 500,000 children. 2

> **Even small doses of radioactivity in the body can lead to serious disease and death.**

Ionizing radiation from radioactive decay causes changes in living organisms. These changes can be linked in a chain, and may be reversible or irreversible. These changes lead to different biological consequences.

Biological effects of ionizing radiation can be roughly divided into two stages. The primary stage affects different processes occurring inside a biological organism. The second stage shows the disruption of the entire organism as a consequence of impairing the primary processes.

The majority of the body mass of living organisms is water (H_2O) (about 75%). Water in the body is contained in the cells and in the extracellular space. As any substance, living tissue absorbs energy from radiation. Atoms in the irradiated material may be excited or ionized. The primary processes caused by ionizing radiation in living organisms are largely determined by the absorption of radiation by water. Ionization of water molecules leads to the formation of the free radicals H and OH. In the presence of oxygen, free radicals also form hydroperoxide (HO_2) and hydrogen peroxide (H_2O_2). These two substances are powerful oxidants. In general, substances that are formed in the ionization of the water molecules have a high oxidative activity. They react with molecules of proteins, enzymes and other biological tissue, which changes the biochemical processes in the body. This results in disturbances of the metabolism, decreased activity of enzymes, slowed growth of tissue, and formation of new compounds not characteristic of the organism i.e. toxins. This leads, in turn, to impaired function of the body as a whole. All this is an indirect effect of ionizing radiation on the body through the ionization of water molecules. The direct effect of ionizing radiation often causes splitting of protein molecules and other changes.

In the future, under the influence of the modified primary processes in the cells of living organism there are changes that affect the heritable properties. Most sensitive to the effects of ionizing radiation are the cells of the bone marrow, gonads, spleen, and other constantly renewed tissues and organs.

During the last 26 years, since the Chernobyl accident, residents of the contaminated areas have continued to eat locally produced food containing long lasting radionuclides - especially cesium-137 - at levels well above acceptable limits.

Compared to external radiation, the radiation inside the body coming from these radionuclides may be too weak to be measured by classical gauges, usually called Geiger counters. Nevertheless, lowlevel radiation that affects the body from within can cause irreparable damage to the organism over time. To capture lowlevel radiation you need a device that is designed just for this purpose - such as the spectrometer for human radiation (SHR) developed by the Belrad Institute.

One of the properties that can be clearly observed about cesium-137 is its uneven accumulation in the body's various organs. Studies have shown that the concentration of cesium-137 is ten to one hundred times higher in certain vital organs (kidneys, liver, heart) than the average level in the entire body.[13] For example: at an average level of 50 Bq/kg of Cs-137 for the entire body, levels in the kidneys reach 3000-4000 Bq/kg and levels in the heart reach 1000 Bq/kg. In other words, the measurement of the average dose does not provide enough information: one must know how it is

---

[13] [13] Y.I.Bandazhevsky, *ChronicCs-137 incorporation in childrens organs*, Swiss Medical Weekly, 2003; 133: 488-490

distributed in the body. Quantities accumulated in the body are extremely small, a 1.3 ng (a nanogram is one billionth gram/ 10^{-9}) portion of cesium-137 corresponds to a suggested notional total dose of 4000 Bq (100 Bq/kg in a child weighing 40 kg). They are therefore difficult to track with biochemical methods, as opposed to the damage caused by their inherent radioactivity. It is thus not the chemical toxicity of cesium that affects human metabolism at this low dose, but the radiotoxicity caused by the radioactive isotope.

The severity of pathological processes in vital organs is directly proportional to the amount of cesium-137 accumulated in the body. The larger the amount, the greater the damage will be to the organs.

> **In a population, children and youth are the most vulnerable when it comes to radiation.**

The increase in the number of birth defects in children whose mothers did not receive special attention during pregnancy is one of the consequences of the chronic low-dose radiation emitted by the radionuclides stuck inside their bodies. We see an increase in the incidence of diabetes (diabetes mellitus), chronic diseases of the digestive system, respiratory system, autoimmune diseases, allergies and cases of thyroid cancer and malignant blood disorders. These autoimmune diseases indicate that the cells responsible for neutralizing infectious germs and viruses or cancerous cells, are instead attacking healthy cells in certain organs such as those that produce insulin in the pancreas. This self-destruction is the basis for severe diabetes. The incidence of children's- and teens-tuberculosis is growing. It is among the residents of Gomel that growth is highest, confirming the radioactive factor to be responsible of impairing the immune system, which leads further to impaired resistance to tuberculosis bacteria and other infections.

> **It is possible to prevent the pathogenic effect of radioactive contamination.**

The effect of radionuclides in the human body, primarily cesium-137, has been studied in its various aspects as part of research on the cardiovascular system, visual organs, lymphatic system, reproductive system, the condition of the tissues, metabolism and blood system.

It turns out that the cardiovascular system is the most sensitive to high levels of radioactive cesium. The frequency of errors in cardiac function is directly related to the amount of cesium-137 absorbed. Heart failure has been observed in 18% of children contaminated with less than 5 Bq/kg, in 65% of children contaminated from 11 to 26 Bq/kg and in 87% of children contaminated with more than 74 Bq/kg of cesium-137. [14]

The fact that the cardiovascular system is affected by internal radiation from radioactive cesium is revealed through the increase in the number of people affected by severe heart disease or elevated blood pressure occurring already in childhood-years.

Our sight is also very sensitive to radioactivity. Among the most common diseases related to visual disorders, we can men-

---

[14] [14] G.S. Bandazhevskaya, V.B.Nesterenko, V.I Babenko, T.V. Yerkovich, Y.I Bandazhevsky, *Relationship between Cesium (^{137}Cs)load, cardiovascular symptoms, and source of food i "Chernobyl" children – preliminary observations after intake of oral apple pectin,* Swiss Medical Weekly, 2004; 134: 725-729

tion cataracts, degeneration of the vitreous (between the lens and the retina). A high dose of radiation from outside leads to degeneration of the retina that begins after a latency period of several years, which then leads to blindness a few years later – as occurred to many of the liquidators[15]. Studies document the correlation between the amount of internal radionuclides and incidence of cataracts. It is important to emphasize that a reduction of radioactive cesium levels inside the organism removes the described diseases. Stated another way, it is possible to alleviate eye disease by increasing the excretion of cesium from the organism. The situation isn't completely hopeless.

Radioactive cesium can be accumulated in the organs of the abdomen: liver, spleen, intestinal walls, pancreas and kidneys. It can cause severe damage to the cells of these organs.

The immune system is significantly affected by ionizing radiation, so that the resilience of the body falls. As in the preceding cases, this destruction is proportional to the absorbed radiation dose.

Radioactive substances that are absorbed by tissue affect the blood system, nervous system and reproductive organs.

Medical research shows that the severity of damage caused in the organism varies with the amount of radionuclides absorbed and the duration of the contamination. Sometimes the damage caused is irreversible. But still, you should know and remember

---

[15] Liquidators: the name given in the former Soviet Union to civilian and military personnel who were set to clean up the site during the Chernobyl disaster in 1986

that there are methods to reduce radiation exposure to a minimum.

THE MEASUREMENT OF RADIOLOGICAL CONTAMINATION IN FOOD

After the Chernobyl disaster, a system for monitoring radiation in the human environment was established in Belarus under the supervision of ministries and local authorities. It is concerned with radiation in the air, soil, water resources, forests and food. The most important of these in the current circumstances is monitoring radiation in food, because most of the radiation people receive is from internal radiation resulting from people's food intake.

The Health Ministry (Minzdrav) responsible for the control of vegetable gardens and private farms as well as harvest from the forest has not been effective in this work. The reasons for this include lack of vehicles, lack of fuel, lack of trained specialists and lack of suitable measuring instruments.

Since 1990, the independent Belrad Institute has been monitoring the amount of cesium-137 in vegetables produced in gardens and private agriculture. For this purpose Belrad has created Local Centres for Radiological Control (LCRC) in cooperation with local authorities such as schools and health clinics. This was done with financial support from the Chernobyl Committee. These LCRC's have been set up in the largest villages in the Chernobyl region including the districts around Gomel, Brest and Mogilev. There is also an LCRC in the Minsk region (70 km from the capital). Unfortunately, the local government seized these independent centres and most are now shut down. Still the Belrad Institute managed to create a database with more than 320 000 measurements of cesium-137 in locally produced foods, all taken in LCRCs.

The analysis of these data shows that 15% of milk samples contain cesium-137 above permissible levels (111 Bq/ l according to the standards of 1996 and 100 Bq/ l according to those from 1999). More than 80% of products from the forest (mushrooms, berries, wild game, fish, etc.), also contain cesium-137 above permissible levels. The annual internal radiation dose in children from rural areas is due to milk (60%) and forest products (40%), which contain a high content of cesium-137.

> **Particularly hazardous foods are game, mushrooms, [blue]berries.**

Regional health centres (stations for hygiene and epidemiology) also inspect foodstuffs originating from the private sector. These centres found heavy contamination levels in local products. Radiation values in hundreds of measurements of mushrooms between 1999 and 2007 have proven to be above the official guideline levels in 100% of the samples in the areas around Yelsk, Narovlia, Braguine and up to 80% of the samples in Rechitsa region.

High levels of cesium-137 in milk poses a risk of high-level accumulation in children and is the main reasons for the steep deterioration of their health.

HOW TO CONDUCT RADIOLOGICAL MONITORING OF FOOD?

Radiation from radionuclides in contaminated food is too weak to be detected by ordinary Geiger counters. It cannot be detected against background radiation of the surroundings. To assess the radiation it is necessary to study radiation from different sources isolated from each other. Food is monitored using a special device called radiometer. For example, the local LCRC's used an automated gamma radiometer (model RUG-92 and RUG-92M) to measure the level of radioactive cesium in foods, seed and in animal feed.

(See page 39: radiation detector operated by two children trained by Belrad Institute)

A radiometer consists of a container shielded against the background radiation by a thick lead-case, a detector, measurement electronics and a display. The item to be measured is placed in the container where the detector is mounted (the volume should be between one-quarter and one litre). If the product to be measured contains radionuclides, this will be registered by the detector and the result of the measurement will be displayed on a electronic monitor.

The units of measurement are becquerel per kilogram (Bq/kg) for solid or granular products, and becquerel per litre (Bq/l) for liquids. To know whether the product is suitable for consumption, one simply compares the results with the official limits established for food and drinking water (known as RDU-99). In theory, the product can be consumed if it contains less radionuclides than the established norm.

However, the specialists in the Belrad Institute consider any amount of radioactive cesium in the body as dangerous: it is important to know that any new radiation source finding its way into the body simply adds to that already there and that RDU-99's limit values are only indicative. In the opinion of the experts from Belrad, the limiting value for children should be no more than 37 Bq/kg for all foods, not only for products intended for infants (see table page 36).

A natural question, when you live in contaminated areas, is to know where you can check the production from your own vegetable garden, the farm, from the forest or from the store.

It is necessary to continuously monitor radiation contamination in all food products in the Chernobyl area, especially milk and products from the forest. If cows graze in the forest or in sodden meadows, their milk must always be checked. Whenever cows change grazing or forage, their milk must be checked. It is logical to check harvested forage. Mushrooms and berries must be checked. It may be possible to identify areas where one can pick mushrooms and berries that can be eaten after they are treated properly.

Control foodstuffs!

A gamma-radiameter for measurement of radioactivity in foodstuffs, with detector electronics, control and shield.

Advised limits for cesium-137 i foodstuffs (Bq/kg or Bq/l) by October 2013

Foodstuff	Threashhold limits in Belarus (RDU-99)	Limits in Japan after Fukushima feb.'12 *	Limits in Norway feb.'13 **	Limits EU/ produced in EU*** until 31.03.2014	Original limits in EU/ produced in EU ****	Limits USA
drinking water	10	10			1000	1200
liquid foodstuffs				100	500	
food in general, including diary products		100			1250	1200
milk		50			1000	1200
other foodstuffs except fodstuff of minor importance				100	500	
milk and wholemilk products	100		370			
milk and milk products				50	200	
concentrated milk, condensed milk	200					
curd	50					
wheycheese and spread	50					
butter	100					

     After the Nuclear Accident – V.Babenko

Foodstuff	Threashhold limits in Belarus (RDU-99)	Limits in Japan after Fukushima feb.'12 *	Limits in Norway feb.'13 **	Limits EU/ produced in EU*** until 31.03.2014	Original limits in EU/ produced in EU ****	Limits USA
meat and meat products: cattle and sheep	50					
pork, poultry and- products	180	}100				
bread and bread products	40					
potatoes and root vegetables	80					
flour, semolina, sugar	60					
Plant oils	40					
animal fat and margarine	100					
vegetables and root crops	100	100				
fruits	40					
berries cultivated	70					
preserved: vegetables, fruits, cultivated berries	74					
wild berries and fruits, jams	185					
fresh mushrooms	370		}3000			
dried mushrooms	2500					
ALL products for baby food	37	50	370	50	400? 200?	1200
reindeer, game, freshwater fish			3000			
other foodstuffs	370	100	600			

* Japan sets stricter limits for foodstuffs 12.Feb.2012, 20 times more stringent than in the U.S. and the EU:

http://www.yomiuri.co.jp/dy/national/T120217006336.htm

** Cesium-137 accumulates in the Norwegian dairy product *brown cheese*. For the finished product not to exceed the limit of 600 becquerels/kg, only milk below 50 becquerels/kg is to be used in production.

*** Limit only applies to items manufactured in the EU; on imports of Japanese goods Japanese values are used.

**** The EU Commission put a directive in force that adapts European values to the strict Japanese values: Japanese authorities lowered values drastically April 1, 2012. EU took over the low values, initially valid until 31 March 2014 (EU Directive 996/2012). http://www.bfs.de/de/kerntechnik/unfaelle/fukushima/strahlens chutz_europa.html/print

Vladimir Babenko, co-director
of the Belrad Institute,
author of this booklet

Prof. Vassily Nesterenko
nuclear- / reactor physician
founder of the Belrad Institute

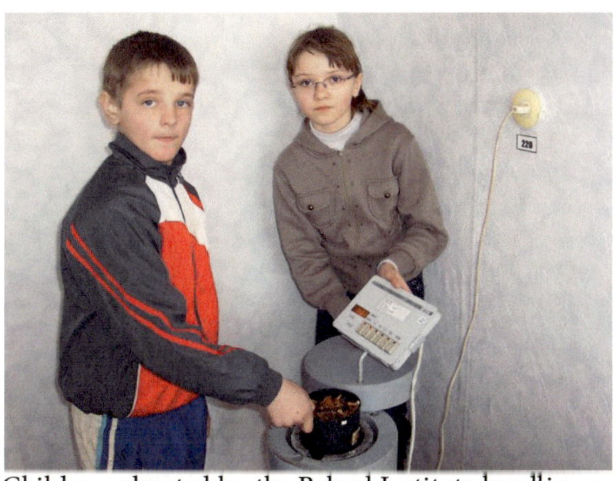

Children educated by the Belrad Institute handling a detector of radioactivity

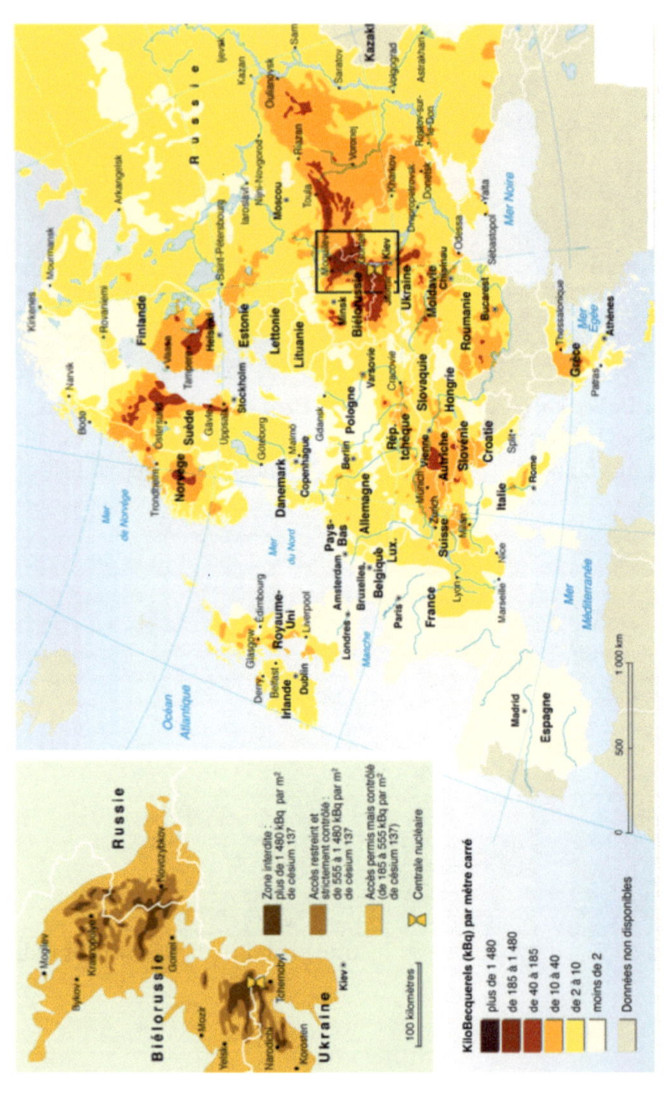

MAP SHOWING THE CONTAMINATION OF EUROPE CAUSED BY THE CHERNOBYL ACCIDENT (Gratification Le Monde Diplomatique)

   After the Nuclear Accident – V.Babenko

The situation in Belarus

Belarus is the country that has suffered the highest amount of fallout from the Chernobyl accident (70% of the source term). This contamination affects a quarter of its territory and nearly 2 million people. The contaminated areas are classified according to four levels of soil contamination. National management of the consequences of the Chernobyl accident (financial aid, resettlement policy, etc...) then depends on the status of the territory in question.

Zones	Level of soil-contamination* in Ci/km^2		
	Cs-137	Sr-90	Pu-238, 239, 240
Zone 1 : periodic radiological control	1 - 5	0,15 – 0,5	0,01 – 0,02
Zone 2 : right to migrate	5 - 15	0,5 – 2	0,02 – 0,05
Zone 3 : right to resettle	15 - 40	2 – 3	0,05 – 0,1
Zone 4 : compulsory and immediate resettlement	> 40	> 3	> 0,1

Table 1 : Definition of contamination-zones (Belarus law of 1991)
* 1 Ci/km^2 (1 Curie per square kilometer) = 37 000 Bq/m^2

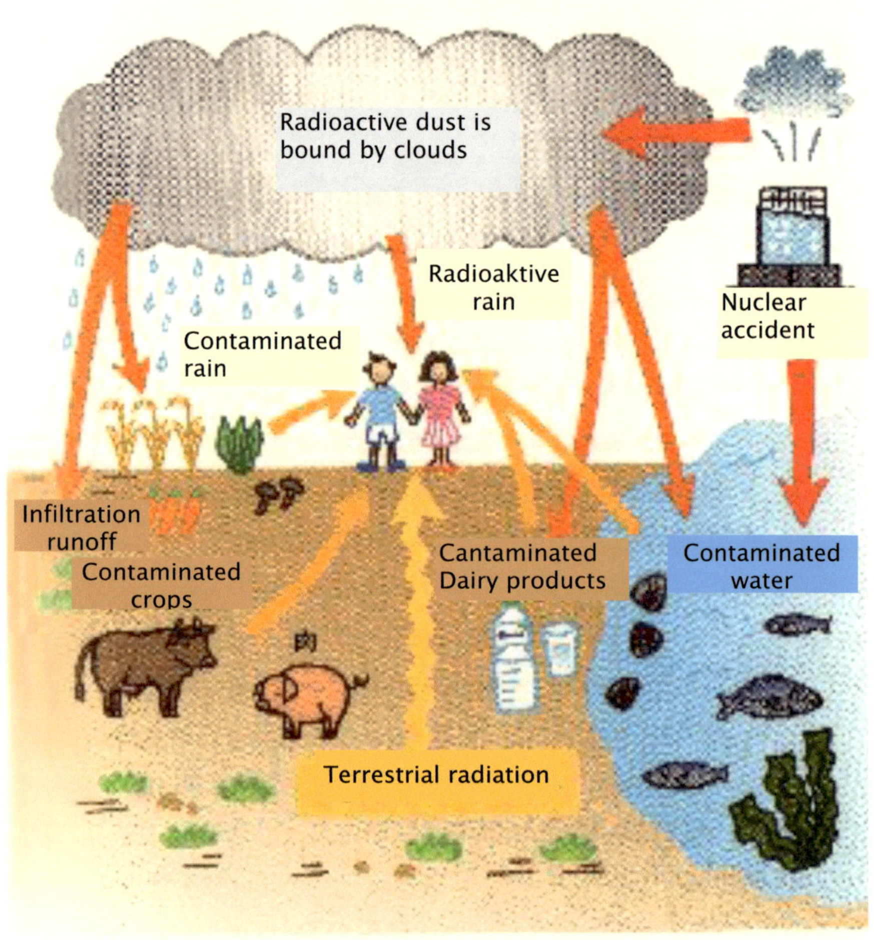

Radioactive dust is bound by clouds
Radioaktive rain
Nuclear accident
Contaminated rain
Infiltration runoff
Contaminated crops
Cantaminated Dairy products
Contaminated water
Terrestrial radiation

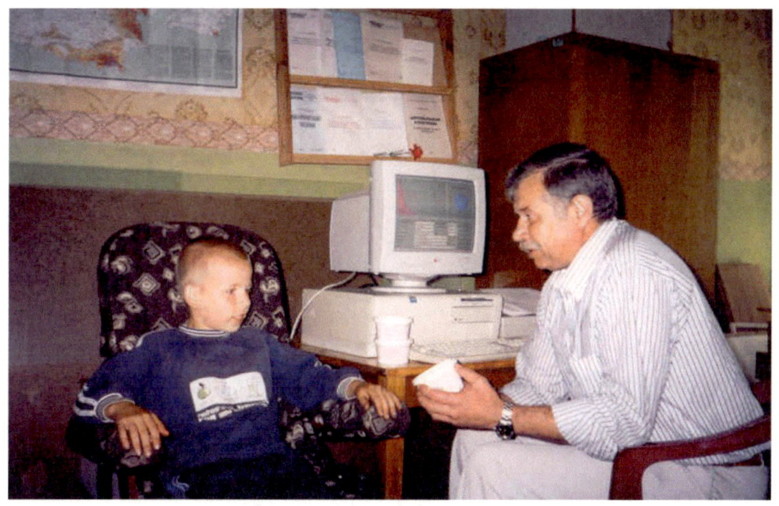

Monitoring radiation in childrens bodies

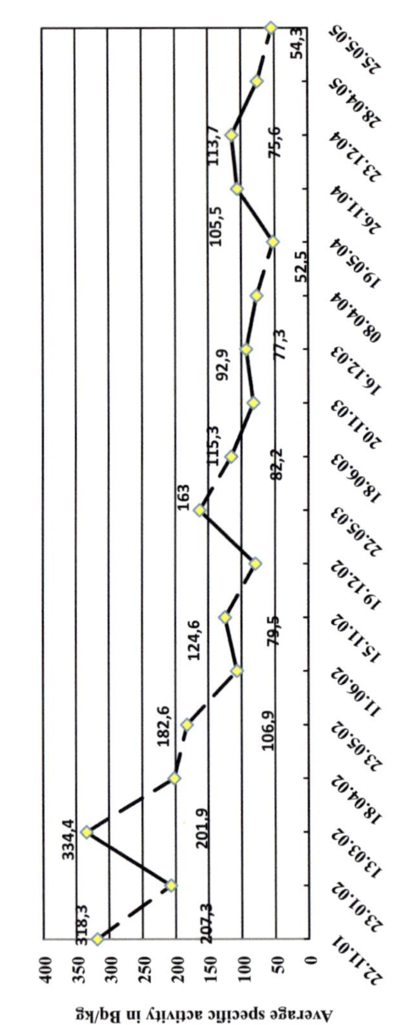

– – – – Period under treatment with Vitapect: note that it always produces a net decrease in the average body contamination of the children. Without treatment the average level of contamination would be higher.

After the Nuclear Accident – V.Babenko

Course of radioactivity levels in the body of V.Ch., born in 1995, student at School No. 1 in Tschetschersk, Gomel area.

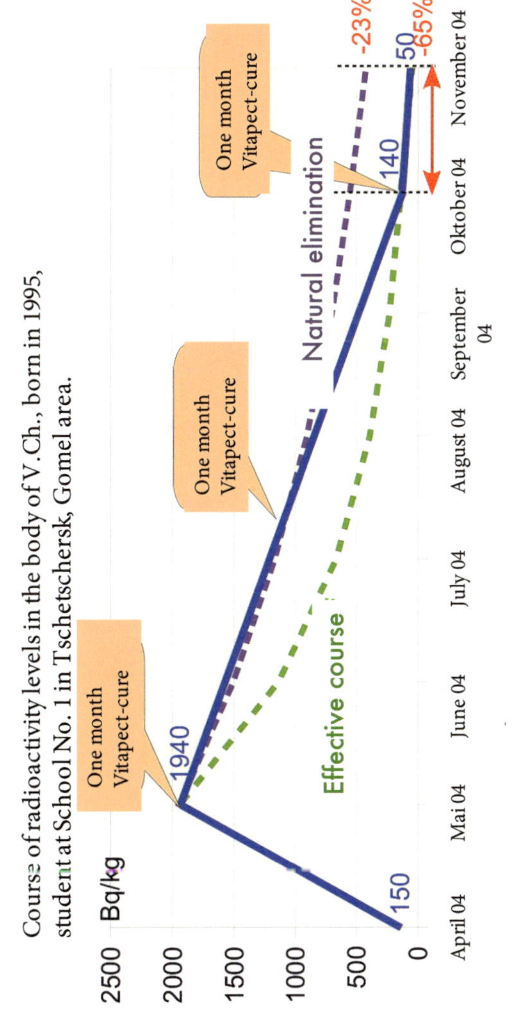

The graphic shows that Vitapect rescued a girl after a hazardous contamination accident. An individual detector measurement is absolutely necessary to find the people who should be foremost in the queue of individuals that must be treated.

MEASURING RADIOACTIVITY IN THE HUMAN BODY

In the previous section, we have just gone through how radionuclides enter the human body and what effects they have on the organism. The longer the radionuclides stay in the body, the greater the damage that is done. Consequently, it is very important to detect as early as possible those children and adults with hazardous accumulations of radionuclides in their body. Why start with the kids? The fact is that the accumulation of radionuclides in their bodies is much faster than in adults. With an identical diet, children absorb a dose two to four times higher than adults.

One might ask why we are still talking about children. Haven't 26 years passed since the Chernobyl disaster? The answer is that one may have lived without radionuclides in the body for a long time and then suddenly become contaminated by a single meal. The sooner one discovers such contamination, the sooner one can take steps to accelerate the excretion of radionuclides from the organism.

In the measurement of radiation in the human body, we are interested in the kind of radionuclides and how much of each type is present. Measuring radioactivity in the body needs a special device called a Spectrometer for Human Radiation (SHR). Some parents fear that measuring contamination in their children by means of an SHR can pose a health risk. We can reassure those: Unlike fluoroscopy and X-ray measurements, measurements with the SHR are not dangerous. The spectrometer is a passive device, which measures only the radiation emitted by the body.

(Photo page 43: Measurement of body radiation of a child.)

So, what is a SHR and how can it be used to measure radiation?

SPECTROMETER FOR HUMAN RADIATION (SHR) AND HOW IT WORKS

The automated spectrometer for internal radiation from humans, "Screener-3M", is designed to determine the activity of gamma emitting radionuclides in the human body and to identify the dose resulting from that activity. The "Screener 3M" consists of a diagnostic chair, a PC, and a control source.

The device looks like an armchair. Let us assume that the person in the chair has a body contaminated with a certain amount of radioactive isotopes that emit gamma radiation. In the back of the chair, protected from ambient radiation by a lead casing, there are crystals of sodium iodide (NaI) acting as detectors (scintillation counters). The moment a radionuclide decays in the subject, it releases a gammaray, which, in half of the cases, will reach the detector to cause a flash of light there. This light is detected by a optical detector called a "photomultiplier tube" or PMT.

The electrical signal from the PMT is, in turn, processed and sent to the computer. Special software processes the information and displays the result on the screen. One can estimate the number of disintegrations in the person's body in relation to the number of flashes. Each nuclide disintegrates with a specific energy corresponding to a defined brightness in the detector. In this way, one can distinguish the various radionuclides that produce gamma-radiation in the body: cesium, cobalt, potassium, manganese, etc.

The most common contaminant found in the population affected by radiation from Chernobyl is cesium-137. This radionuclide constitutes the main source of internal radiation from within the body. The people that we measure using the SHR are always interested in the range of results we get; is that a lot? is it little? What are the permissible values?

The spectrometer measures "specific activity", that is, the number of disintegrations per second per mass unit (typically Becquerel per kg or Bq/kg). However, the legal limit according to Belarusian law sets the upper limit for radiation exposure in terms of dose (typically measured in Sieverts per year or Sv/yr).

To protect the people living in contaminated areas, is it enough to know the amount of external radiation they receive (typically measured in mSv/ year)? Or must one also know the amount of radionuclides a body contains (internal radiation) measured in the whole body (typically measured in Bq)? Which measurements are most important?

To protect people from radiation it is not enough to know the dose of external radiation, to which they are exposed. In Belarus today, more than 90% of the radiation exposure comes from internal sources. In 1992, when measurement of radiation doses began, the focus was on contamination in milk and potatoes, which were then seen as the most important foodstuffs with regard to contamination. The total dose of radiation received was calculated from a series of 10-15 samples of these foods. The village's population varies, from a few people to a few hundred and even thousands. The term used in the register "public radiation dose" is absolutely not correct and can NOT be used to protect a particular person. For an objective assessment of the presence and

    After the Nuclear Accident – V.Babenko

amount of any of radionuclides in a human organism, it is necessary to screen the population using a SHR (Spectrometer of Human Radiation). That is the only way to get individual and objective information about the level of radionuclides accumulated in an individual at a given time. It is on the basis of this information that radiation protection measures can be determined, such as, for example, the need for an extensive medical examination.

***

Is it more important to estimate the "radiation dose" someone has received or to measure the amount of absorbed radionuclides?

To estimate an absorbed radiation dose can have a certain scientific justification. In this case, we are talking about gamma rays. The energy of gamma rays is partially absorbed by the organism. Each organ shows a different susceptibility to this influence, which can be expressed in an "impact coefficient". The combination of all contributions to each organ and from each of the calculated doses will together provide the absorbed dose.

However this concept is inappropriate to describe the damage caused by internal radiation. Here is an image that allows us to understand the difference: we can warm us comfortably in front of a campfire but the same amount of heat could also have been received by swallowing a glowing piece of coal ... which is not as comfortable. The absorbed radionuclides behave like glowing bits of coal: a big damage in the immediate vicinity, which decreases with increasing distance from the source. The only measurement that can give an idea of the possible effects of radioactive contamination is one that shows the amount of radionuclides in the body. This assessment is demonstrated by the basic studies of

Prof. Youry Bandashevsky, Vassily Nesterenko and Dr. Galina Bandashevskaya. They have shown that there is a contamination threshold of 20 Bq/ kg body weight of cesium-137. Beyond this, we see a significant increase in heart rhythm disorders. One suspects that the other diseases developed by contaminated children are also triggered at a similar threshold of contamination.

***

What is the relationship between the radiation level in a contaminated area and the amount of radionuclides in people's bodies?

Belrad Institute has conducted a study of the correlation between contamination levels of cesium in a region and the amount of cesium accumulated in the bodies of inhabitants by relying on measurements from 100 locations in the Gomel area. *No connection at all was found between these values.* If one assumes that the amount of accumulated radioactive cesium in a body depends on the surrounding contamination levels, one would expect that all residents of a given area would show similar cesium values. But this is simply not the case. In one location, residents have cesium levels, which vary by up to a factor of several hundred.

The hypothesis of associating surrounding contamination and the amount of radionuclides in the inhabitants bodies disregards a multitude of factors covered by the established notion of *risk factors*. These include:

- different contamination levels in different ecosystems

- individual differences of human bodies

- topsoil particle size and soil-type which determine the uptake of radioactive elements in both soil and plants

- the type of residence (accumulation-levels are lower in cities and towns than in rural areas because people in the cities are nourished primarily by food coming from controlled agriculture bought in stores, while people in rural areas eat local products including products gathered from the forest)

- the social and economic status of the family (usually the largest contamination is found in the body of children from large families, from disadvantaged families or from families of single parents)

- the surroundings of the property (if it is surrounded by forests, marsh, pastures, etc.)

- the knowledge and skill of people about living in contaminated environment, growing a vegetable garden and cooking food in a way that lowers the radioactive contents of the food

- the opportunities or lack thereof, to add soil-fertilizers, including potassium (if the soil lacks potassium, cesium replaces it and enters the human body through the food chain)

- the amount of food harvested in the forest varying from year to year (at the beginning of the millennium, 2001, 2004 and 2008 were the most abundant years for mushrooms, which resulted in elevated cesium levels in residents)

- public measures such as prohibition of picking berries and mushrooms in very polluted forests

- the season of measurement (analysis show that the highest radiation levels occur in October-November, which is mushroom- and berry-season; then the values decrease until April, before there is a slight increase in May - related to milk cows released on pastures, values falling again to July when berries begin to ripen, then increasing again due to mushrooms, with highest levels in October-November

- if there are hunters in the family (the values of cesium in game around Gomel exceeding hundreds of times the acceptable limits);

- the information available to the public through the media

- parental concern for good health for their children and the practical measures they take toward that goal.

So we have different units, depending on what we measure:
- The amount of radioactivity: Bq-becquerel
- The energy absorbed: J/kg = Gy – gray
- The corresponding/ effective radiation dose for a person: Sv – sievert

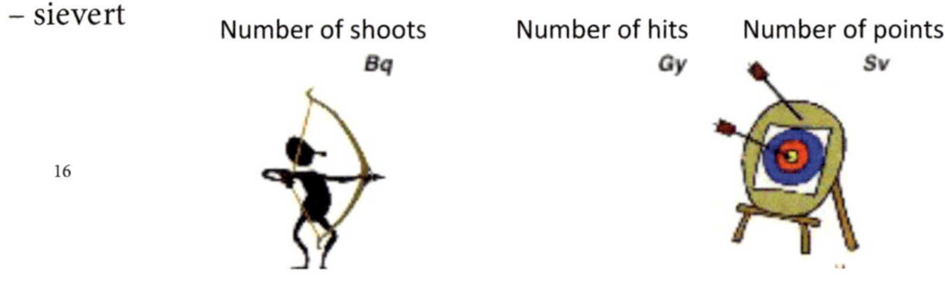

16

---

[16] www.ntnu.no/documents/2004699/349c929d-b2b6-4ef9-86f7-80e9ad04e033

"Dose" is the energy a body receives from radioactive sources outside the body when one neglects to accurately measure the absorbed amount. To define "dose" begins with measuring the background radiation in becquerels. The objective number of disintegration per second measured by the unit is then subject to a calculation that takes into account the various subjective factors (the impact this type of radiation has on affected body tissues, age, etc.). These factors vary according to different methods, leading to 1mSv never being equal to itself. The law of the Belarusian Republic has established a dose limit of 1mSv/ year, which correspond to a "calculated" dose of internal radiation (the method used by the Ministry of Health) a cesium-137 activity from 361 to 433 Bq/ kg depending on age group.

The Belrad Institute conducts its measurements directly in Becquerel since the radiation source is inside the body. The situation is different for external radiation, which cannot be measured objectively. The Belrad Institute recommends that the following limits for cesium-137 should not be exceeded:

	Threshold value	*Threshold value requiring a cure*
Adults	200 Bq/kg	70 Bq/kg
Children	70 Bq/kg	20 Bq/kg

When it comes to establishing norms, threshold values, etc., responsible institutions are often directed by motives other than public health. Economic factors, as well as political and social factors come into play.

Logical thinking and common sense require the Belrad Institute to advise one and the same radiation level for both children and adults: zero Bq per kg body weight.

Cesium-137 is an element that does not occur naturally in the human body. If it shows up in one's body, it must be due to contamination of soil and water, which, in turn, may result from radioactive fallout (nuclear tests, nuclear accidents at Chernobyl or Fukushima) or radioactive waste (waste from the nuclear industry that was buried or released in rivers, lakes or oceans, contaminated water from the nuclear plant, etc). Any value other than zero is abnormal.

Regardless of the amount of radioactive cesium detected in the body, it is necessary to take steps to counteract its harmful effects. The following chapters are devoted to such measures. We will see that they are diverse and they require no special investment or governmental decision. To implement them, it is enough to be sufficiently organized and to possess some basic knowledge.

SECOND PART: EATING CLEAN

PREPARING FOOD TO PREVENT RADIATION

One can reduce the content of radionuclides in foodstuffs considerably through proper preparation. However, it is essential to remember that the proposed methods can only be used, when the content of radionuclides does not exceed the recommended limits by more than a factor of two or three. If contamination is tens or hundreds of times higher than recommended, no precautions can make the food edible.

Here an example: In the region of Gomel dried mushrooms were measured to have a specific cesium-137 activity of of 32,000 Bq/kg, exceeding the recommended limit of 2,500 Bq/kg by 13 times. It is obvious that no treatment can make these mushrooms harmless.

> **Cesium-137, the main source of contamination, is water soluble and does not bind to fat. It is these properties that make it possible to remove it from food.**

Treatment of vegetables from the kitchen garden

To prepare the vegetables for cooking, you must begin by removing the parts where the majority of radionuclides have accumulated, meaning those on the surface. When one removes the large cover-leaves from cabbage, the remaining radioactive contamination will be 40 times lower. Removing the green leaves of beets, radishes, turnips, carrots, etc. decreases their radioactive contamination by 5 to 7 times. A washed potato will be two times less radioactive after being peeled. Once threshed and separated from the chaff, grain becomes 10 to 15 times less radioactive.

So here are some simple rules to follow before you eat or cook vegetables:

- Rinse with plenty of water all the fruits and vegetables

- Remove 3 or 4 of the big cabbage leaves

- Brush away the soil and rinse potatoes and root vegetables well

- Cut off 1 to 1.5 cm of the top of the root vegetables

The preservation of vegetables and garden fruits (lacto-fermentation/ sauerkraut, storage in vinegar, etc.) makes it possible to reduce the amount of radioactive particles further, provided that the brines and marinades that the vegetables lie in, are not consumed. There is nothing special about this advice. Every housewife washes and peels vegetables. However, if one lives in a contaminated area, it is vital that it is done particularly thoroughly.

Treatment of milk

By treating milk at home, in our own kitchens, we can free milk from a great deal of contaminating radionuclides: these remain dissolved in the whey. However one must never forget that this whey must not be used; it is not suitable for human consumption.

When separating milk, the cream is 4 to 6 times less contaminated than the milk. In the same manner, cottage cheese you make out of contaminated milk contains 4 to 6 times less radionuclides, white cheese 8 to 10 times less, butter 8 to 10 times less, and clarified butter 90 to 100 times less to the point that you could almost say that it no longer contains any radionuclides.

Let us for instance consider milk that shows a radioactivity of 150 Bq/l of cesium-137, while the threshold value is 100 Bq/l. The radioactivity in cream, separated from the whey will not show more than 25 to 37 Bq/l. Stated another way, the cream can be given to children following those rules.

Treatment of meat

Radioactive cesium adheres especially to soft tissues in animals and concentrates especially in the liver and kidneys, which are filter organs. It is therefore necessary to control butchery. Cesium almost never adheres to the bones – it is rather radioactive strontium, which does so, and it is almost impossible to remove it from there. That is why it is not advisable to prepare broth from bones, or to consume such stock.

Bacon and fat accumulate minimal amounts of radioactive elements. In addition, if you melt pork fat, 95% of cesium remains in bacon while lard is practically pure. Generally, pigs are less contaminated than beef or poultry. In contrast, game meat usually contains very high levels of radionuclides. The values measured in wild game can exceed the limit by tens and hundreds of times. Even if game meat is processed by the methods we recommend, it is unlikely that we can make the meat "clean". In Belarus, this applies especially to the region around Narovlia, Love, Braguine, Khoïniki, Tchetchersk, Vetka, Korma, and Leltch. The Belrad Institute has measured radioactivity in wild boar meat and found values exceeding 55,000 Bq/kg, but the limit is set to 370 Bq/kg for "other foodstuffs". Even if we could reduce the contamination by a factor of 10 through appropriate processing, the result would be meat with 5,500 Bq/kg, ie it is still not suitable for consumption.

To reduce radioactivity in meat, one cuts the meat in small chunks and soaks it in salt water with 2% salt. It must soak for at least 12 hours, changing the brine several times. The longer the meat soaks and the more often the salt water is replaced, the less radionuclides will be left in the meat. Most of the cesium will be removed with the salt water. To prevent the nutritional value disappearing with the salt water, we need to add some vinegar or ascorbic acid, which will slow down the dissolution of proteins.

Unfortunately, the meat is not as tasty after such treatment, but one has no choice. Maybe it's better to skip certain taste sensations in order to protect oneself from radioactivity.

If we cook meat for about ten minutes, about half of radionuclides will be dissolved in the broth: this in turn becomes unfit for use and must be discarded.

Food from the forest: berries and mushrooms

Food from the forest is the most dangerous category of foodstuff. Radioactive fallout is deposited on the forest soil that creates a screen preventing them to go deeper into the ground. Most of the radionuclides stay in the top 3-5cm of the soil. One can also find large concentrations of radionuclides in tree bark, rotten wood, moss and lichens, berries and mushrooms.

Among the least contaminated berries are rowanberries (Sorbus domestica), raspberries and strawberries, among the most contaminated are blueberries, lingonberries, cranberries and especially cloudberries.

Picking wild berries should only be permitted if the cesium-137 contamination in the soil does not exceed 74Bq/m2. In this case it is possible to use a conventional dosimeter: it easily measures the radioactivity of an area. If it is too high, it is likely that all vegetation there is contaminated. If it is low, you can pick berries without risk.

We must pay very special care to mushrooms. We can divide them in four groups according to their ability to accumulate contamination:

Group I, the most dangerous. There we find mushrooms that readily accumulate the highest level of radionuclides: *Xerocomus badius, Lactarius rufus, Lactarius subdulcis, Boletus variegatus, Lactarius deliciosus, Suillus luteus, Suillus bovinus, Rozites caperata.*(Bay Bolete, Rufous Milkcap, Mild Milkcap, *Velvet Bolete,* Saffron Milkcap, Slippery Jack, Bovine Bolete, Gypsy Mushroom). Such mushrooms may not be collected except in areas with less than 37,000 Bq/m2 (= 1Ci/km2) and they must be subjected to systematic radioactivity control.

Group II: mushrooms that concentrate high levels of radionuclides. There we find *Russula adusta, Cantharellus cibarius, Lactarius torminosus, Lactarius turpis, Tricholoma flavovirens, Boletus scaber.* (Winecork Brittlegill, Chanterelle, Woolly

Milkcap, Ugly Milkcap, Yellow Knight, Birch Bolete). These mushrooms are not to be collected when growing on soils contaminated with more than 37,000 Bq/m2 and they must be systematically checked.

Group III, mushrooms that accumulate medium levels of radioactivity. *Armillariella mellea, Boletus edulis, Leccinum versipelle, Tricholoma portentosum, Russula.* (Honey Fungus, Penny Bun / Cep, Orange Birch Bolete, Charbonier/ Sooty Head, Brittlegill). These mushrooms can be gathered on soils that do not exceed 74,000 Bq/km2 in a zone of obligatory control.

Group IV, mushrooms that absorb low levels of radionuclides: *Gyromitra esculenta, Lepista nuda, Agaricus, Lycoperdon, Flammulina velutipies, Pleurotus.* (False Morel, Wood Blewit, Field Mushroom, Puffball, Velvet Shank, Oyster/ Shield). Nevertheless, this group of mushrooms should also be controlled for radioactivity.

If you have gathered mushrooms in a forest that turn out to be heavily contaminated - do not go back there to pick mushrooms again, because the mushrooms there are going to be "dirty" for decades to come.

Preparation of mushrooms

Mushrooms must be prepared in the following manner to decrease the content of radionuclides:

Mushrooms are to be soaked in a saline with 2% kitchen salt for several hours. Mushrooms contaminated with up to 28,000

Bq/kg, picked around Tchetcherk, showed only 2,000 Bq/kg after soaking for 20 hours in saline that had been replaced twice.

Furthermore the amount of radionuclides contained in mushrooms is reduced by boiling them 15-60 min in saline, replaced every 15 minutes. Adding a spoonful of vinegar or citric acid enhances the transfer of radionuclides from mushrooms to water. It is obvious that the mushrooms will have lost some of their original flavour after such treatment - but we must choose: either delectable mushrooms, that are harmful, or dull taste but no danger.

One must know that the mushroom's hat is more strongly contaminated than the foot, it is therefore recommended to remove mushroom hats.

You may only dry *uncontaminated* mushrooms, because drying does not diminish the radioactivity, on the contrary - it becomes more concentrated. If a kilogram of fresh mushrooms contains 250 Bq/kg of cesium, the specific activity is of 250 Bq/kg. By decreasing the mass 10 times, we still retain the same amount of radionuclides distributed in a ten times smaller mass. The specific mass activity is then 2,500 Bq/kg.

Let us emphasize an important thing regarding the recommended limits: these are made on the basis of average food intake. One assumes that dried mushrooms constitute only a small proportion of food intake of an average person and that is why the limit is set at such a high level as 2500 Bq/kg. However, can we compare the amount of mushrooms eaten by the average resident in the city of Minsk, Belarus' capital, and the amount eaten by the inhabitants of the forests surrounding Braguine, Love or Narovlia? From immemorial times the inhabitants of these regions have dried mushrooms in the traditional way for winter, mushrooms they then eat in large quantities. Since radionuclides *accumulate* in the body, the official limit is not valid for these residents. It is not easy to change eating habits from one day to the next, but since 1986, this is unfortunately necessary. Every time you put a plate of fried mushrooms in front of a child, remind yourself that this meal can shorten the life of the child or cause the child to grow into a sick adult. Your future and that of your children is largely dependent on you, and how you manage your family's nutrition.

BASIS FOR BALANCED NUTRITION

Our body is constantly interacting with the environment. All signals, that our central nervous system receives, come from the environment. Food intake is one of the decisive factors in this interaction: food comes from the environment into the body, where it participates in all vital processes. Food has a direct impact on both the central nervous and the peripheral nervous system's condition, and thereby affects the whole body.

To avoid absorption of radioactive isotopes of the chemical elements which the body needs to live and function, it is necessary that our cells have enough of these element's stable isotopes available. That is how a lack of stable iodine, which is essential for the thyroid gland to function, causes the body to absorb radioactive iodine. Thus we see that one way to protect the organism from radioactive contamination is to nourish ourselves in a balanced way, so that the body is not deprived of any essential elements.

In order to eat in a balanced manner, we need to know what role the various nutrients play in our body, and we must have a clear idea of what our body needs - depending on age, occupation, climate and social conditions.

Proteins

Proteins are the basic elements of life and cells: every living cell, every tissue in the organism, is mostly composed of proteins. For the body's tissues to live, grow and renovate, a continuous supply of protein is needed.

Among the various proteins in food, some are more important than others. Their chemical compositions are very similar to the body's own proteins, containing all the necessary elements (amino acids) to create these. Others are composed in a manner that is more dissimilar to proteins in the human body, and are thus less valuable.

We shall emphasise proteins with high nutritional value such as those found in fish, meat, milk, eggs and certain vegetables: cabbage crops, potatoes and legumes (peas, beans, green beans, etc.).

Among the cereals rich in proteins, the most nutritious are oats, rice and buckwheat. Millet, barley and semolina are much less nutritious sources of proteins.

Fats and carbohydrates

Fats and carbohydrates are our main energy sources and define the caloric content of foods. In addition, they have a protective role for proteins, because if there's enough fat and carbohydrates in the organism, proteins degrade to a lesser extent.

Fat (= lipids) may be stored in the human body not only when they are found abundantly in the consumed food, but also when the food contains a high proportion of carbohydrates. Until recently fats from animal sources were considered to be the most useful, since they contain a larger part of fat-soluble vitamins than vegetable oils. However, recent research has shown that polyunsaturated fatty acids, which we find more of in vegetable oils, are vital.

It is therefore most reasonable to have different types of fat on the menu. Vegetable oils must be part of the nutrition for young children, school children and adults.

Vegetable oils are favourable for the elderly and people suffering from cardiovascular diseases.

Vegetable products, grains and cereals, fruits and vegetables are particularly rich in carbohydrates. As for animal products, milk contains a certain amount of carbohydrate (in the form of lactose). Carbohydrates can be found in foods in the form of starch or various sugars, all absorbed very easily by the human body.

When we have to provide carbohydrates quickly in case of sudden heart failure, great exhaustion or insulin shock, we provide sugar in the form of glucose, injected directly into the blood by intravenous infusion. Normally, our body's need for carbohydrates is mainly satisfied in the form of starch and only a small portion as sugar.

In addition to proteins, fats and carbohydrates, nutrition provides our body with vitamins and mineral salts.

Vitamins

Some vitamins are water-soluble such as C and B vitamins, others are fat-soluble.

Vitamins are as indispensable to us as all the other substances the human body is made up of. The deficiency of a vitamin can lead to dysfunction in individual organs, or the whole organism. Their role is extremely complex. All vitamins are interdependent. The deficiency of one type of vitamins can inhibit the body making use of others.

Vitamin C or ascorbic acid is necessary for the growth of young bodies, it increases endurance and resistance to infectious diseases and external stresses (cold, heat, high and low pressure, etc.). Lack of vitamin C manifests itself through fatigue, drowsiness, dizziness, irritability and a clearly reduced ability to work.

Vitamin C is found in fruits, berries, fresh vegetables, mainly in cabbage and swedes, but also in raddishes, shallots, spinach, lettuce, parsley and sorrel (lat. *Rumex*). Among fruits with the highest vitamin C content we find: lemons, oranges, tangerines, sour apples; among berries: blackcurrants, redcurrants, strawberries, mulberries, cloudberries.

Vitamin C is broken down quickly by boiling, exposure to high temperatures, and exposure to oxygen in the air. To retain most of its good qualities, we recommend some rules to follow:

1) When boiling, add the vegetables to boiling water and be careful not to go below the boiling point but do not boil them too hard either. Do not let them cook too long and do not let vegetables stand on a hot plate or in a warm room afterwards.

2) Do not use a metal cutter or strainer for making purees or finely chopped meat, instead use a wooden chopper, masher or spoon.

3) Use peeled or cooked vegetables immediately.

4) Eat soups and vegetables immediately after they are cooked.

B-vitamins: vitamin B_1 (thiamine), B_3 (nicotinic acid) and B_2 (riboflavin) are those we know most about. Lack of one of these in the body can cause problems in both blood- and nervous systems. B-vitamin deficiency disturbs the normal activity in muscle function and digestive system. B_1 is water-soluble and resistant to oxidation and heat. B_1 is found in yeast, rye and whole grain breads, furthermore in meat, milk, starch, nuts and green vegetables.

B_3 vitamins protect the organism against pellagra, severe vitamin deficiency affecting the skin, the digestive system and the nervous system. One can find B_3 vitamins in yeast, dark bread, liver, meat, fish, milk, cabbage crops and tomatoes.

B_2 vitamins have a crucial role in the work of the digestive system, and as well as vitamin A, for the eyesight. We find them in the same products as B_3 vitamins.

B_6 vitamins (pyrodoxine) is important for the metabolism, more precisely, the metabolism of proteins. Folic acid and vitamin B_{12} are important to different organs and is used to treat anemia. Liver is the main source of B_6, B_{12} and folic acid.

Vitamin A is a group of fat-soluble vitamins. They are crucial for the growing organism because they contribute to the development of the skeleton. Vitamin A- protects the mucous membranes of the respiratory and digestive system. Vitamin A deficiency affects eyesight, We find vitamin A in butter, milk, egg yolk, liver - mainly in fish liver.

Carrots, spinach, salads and different leaves contain a lot of carotene, which is converted to A vitamin in our body.

Vitamin D is essential for children but also for adults, especially those who do not get enough sun.

E-vitamins are required for cell division. They are very widely distributed in nature, we finds them in animal products and also in many vegetables.

Minerals

Different mineral substances play a role in building the human body. They each have their function in our metabolism and affect the development of the various systems and organs. Calcium, magnesium and phosphorus form the basis for bones. Iron, which is a component of blood haemoglobin, is needed to transport oxygen to tissues and organs. Finally, sodium and potassium are water regulating and help keep the body's acid-base balance in equilibrium.

Water

Water is the body's main ingredient. All complex processes in the human body's life take place in a moist environment. (See also p. 28 to understand the importance of supplying our body with water, free from radioactivity).

PART THREE: LIFE CONTINUES

PRODUCTS BASED ON PECTIN

Just as it does with other harmful substances, the human organism secretes radionuclides through the kidneys, liver and gastrointestinal tract. If we don't accelerate this process with suitable means, it will take 90 to 150 days for an adult, and depending on age, 15 to 75 days for a child to secrete half of the absorbed cesium-137. In contaminated environments, although they are within the "acceptable limits", the population is continually exposed to the influence of their own radioactively contaminated organism. While absorbed radionuclides are gradually excreted, living in contaminated zones will result in new radionuclides adding up to those previously absorbed.

To reduce the harmful effects of contamination, it is necessary to help the body to excrete radionuclides faster. To this end, we use products based on pectin. We want to emphasize that these pectin products are not drugs - they are food supplements that consist of only natural ingredients. The main component is pectin. This is a substance found in fruits and vegetables. Citrus plants - lemons, oranges, tangerines – contain the most. But there is also much pectin in apples and beets. Pectin is formed of large molecules that have the ability to bind and thereby bring harmful substances out of the human body. The Institute for Clinical Research in Radiological Medicine and Endocrinology (hormone producing glands and hormones) recommends:

Adults	1-2 teaspoons 2-3 times a day dissolved in a glass of water, tea, compote, juice or other beverage.
Child	1 teaspoon 2 times daily

The duration of such a rehabilitation cure is 3 weeks twice a year, in very contaminated areas 3-4 times annually.

In its practical work with people in contaminated areas the Belrad Institute uses its own product it has developed itself: Vitapect- a dietary supplement based on apple pectin, available in the form of a vitamin drink or pills. The product is certified by the state health-authorities in the Republic of Belarus, and Belrad has permission to manufacture, use and sell Vitapect products.

Vitapect consists of apple powder that is enriched with pectin and vitamins B2, B6, B12, C, E and β-carotene, folic acid, trace elements (potassium, selenium, zinc), lactose and citric acid in amounts according to the recommendations of medical institutions. It contains no preservatives or artificial colourings.

To accelerate the release of radionuclides there is also a product called Belosorb II in Belarus. It is an absorbent in powder form (activated charcoal) containing not more than 3% inorganic impurities.

Yablopekt is a product produced in Dniepropetrovsk (Ukraine). It is made of pectin pills based on apple pectin, which also contains citric acid, sodium bicarbonate (baking soda), sweeteners and vitamins C, E, B1, B2, and β-carotene.

In addition, we find the product Medetopec in Belarus, produced by the Franco-German company Sanofy. It is produced from plant fibres and Spirulina. Fito-Splat and Spirofit are produced by algae and supplied by various foreign companies.

Each of these products has its advantages and disadvantages. Yablopekt for example, contains sodium bicarbonate, which is not recommended to be consumed daily for a whole month (as long as a cure lasts). The advantage of Yablopekt is the content of pectin and vitamins. Belosorb II based on activated carbon promoting the excretion of radionuclides in a good way, but at the same time it transports essential trace elements out of the body, including selenium, it can therefore only be used in limited amounts (some pinches). Vitapect has several advantages: it consists of apple pectin and contains vitamins and trace elements, including selenium.

Since 1996, the Belrad Institute has conducted radiological monitoring of children living in areas contaminated by Chernobyl. Preventive use of pectin products is an integral part of Belrad Institute's work. Prophylactic use of pectin aims to help children's bodies to rid themselves of hazardous radionuclides as quickly as possible in order to reduce the internal radiation contamination. Vitapect is used as absorbent. It is distributed free, but that does not mean that there are no costs involved to produce it. Several charities spend huge amounts of money to give children the opportunity to follow Vitapect cures. Therefore it is important to be aware of the situation's seriousness and always remember, first, that this product helps to remove contamination in children bodies in an efficient manner, and second, that there are people who spend a lot of money from their own pockets to give other people's children the opportunity to receive the cures. Our efforts over many years have proven how efficient the product is. One can remove up to 90% of radionuclides through a cure of 3-4 weeks.

The efficiency of such a cure depends on many factors. If the product is ingested at school or nursery and supervised by health workers or teachers, the effect is relatively good. In some schools the product is only distributed to children, in particular to the largest, without further monitoring. It sometimes happens that the children forget to take it or refuse, saying that they don't like the taste. In such cases there is no decrease in the contamination. Vitapect achieves maximum effect when used in sanatoriums or in rehabilitation centres, under the attentive supervision of physicians and while the children exclusively eat "clean" food. Not all children like the taste of Vitapect so we must explain to them that drugs do not always taste good, but that we, for example, use aspirin, even if it is bitter, to get rid of headaches. Like a drug, Vitapect is there to help, and one must take it, even if one does not like it. If your child has received Vitapect, make sure your child takes it regularly. You should also check that it works: usually a measurement of radioactive nuclides in the body will be made both *before* a cure and, once more, *after* it has ended. Parents can get the results of these measurements in their children schools. If Belrad Institute has conducted surveys of children's bodies in a school, the school is obliged to inform parents about the results.

(Example from Sivitsa School, region of Minsk, p 44)

(Decrease of radioactivity in a girl aged of 9, page 45)

GROWING A VEGETABLE GARDEN IN A CONTAMINATED AREA

Nature does things in a good way: a plant gets what it needs to grow from the soil. But if it does not find a substance it needs, it takes the substance that is most similar.

The chemical properties of cesium-137 are similar to potassium. In radioactive environments, a plant that lacks potassium, will replace it with radioactive cesium. Cesium occupies a vacant niche and in this way, it is taken up by the plant.

Similarly, strontium-90, which is chemically similar to calcium will be absorbed by a plant that lacks calcium.

This property is the basis for the logic and methods to be used in agriculture and gardening to reduce contamination. In general products grown on fields that are treated properly get only slightly contaminated. In any case, you will have to follow the recommendations presented here, in order to guarantee that you will not find any contamination in your food on the dining table. Fertilizing the soil with organic and mineral fertilizers - and lime, if it is *basic* - is therefore vital.

How to care for your kitchen garden:

• Apply lime Dolomite every 4-5 years with about 40-50kg per 100m2.

• Provide artificial garden fertilizer every year:
- 40 g/ m2 for green vegetables, pumpkin, squash
- 60 g/m2 for cabbage-plants

- 90 g/m2 for cucumbers
- 100 g/m2 (or 60 g nitrogen) for root vegetables
- 50 g/m2 for onions, radishes and garlic

• 70 g or 50 g of nitrogen fertilizer per bucket of compost added to ditches and planting holes for tomatoes

• 1.0 to 1.5 kg carbamide (urea) 2-3 kg super phosphate, potassium chloride 2-3 kg / 100m2 for potatoes

• In addition, you need to supply 500-600 kg / 100m2 organic fertilizer (manure, compost soil, compost, peat)

One should not use ash from burning wood from areas with more than 185,000 Bq/m2 of cesium-137. The ash is a kind of concentrate of forest radioactivity. When burning one cubic meter of contaminated wood in logs, the few handfuls of remaining ashes contain nearly the same amount of radionuclides as the original pile. The specific radioactivity in the ash will be hundreds of times greater than in the wood. In contaminated areas it is thus essential to bury the ashes in a suitable site in approximately 1 m deep holes with the bottom sealed with a plastic sheet.

The transfer of radioactive substances from the soil to plants is also dependent on the soil characteristics. The transfer is small in silty loam and rises with clay sand and sandy soil. The transmission is greatest in peat soil.

The concentration of radioactive substances varies according to the plant varieties grown. Here a list of cultivated species set up in ascending order of their ability to accumulate the radioactive isotopes of Cesium: barley grains – rye grains - rye straw - potato – oats - straw of winter rye - fresh forage of mixed grasses and legumes - turnips - fresh forage maize - wheat straw – forage of peas - forage of rapeseed - clover - forage of perennial grain crops - lupines - plants from meadows and natural pastures.

Vegetables, ranked in ascending order of accumulating radioactive substances, are as follows: cabbage - cucumbers - squash - tomatoes - onion - pepper - garlic - potato - beets - carrots - havens - peas - beans - green beans - sorrel / sorrel (Rumex acetosa).

Among berries and fruit: strawberries, white currants, raspberries, apples, pears, sweet cherries, plums and cherries concentrate low amounts of contamination, while red currants, black currants and gooseberries concentrate more radiation.

To minimize the transfer of radionuclides from the soil to garden plants, you must therefore choose wisely what you want to plant.

SUMMARY

This guide to practical radioprotection is based on the experience acquired during the years after the nuclear accident of Chernobyl, of 1986. The guide shows what has happened in these years, what radioactivity is, how it affects human health, how to avoid internalizing it, how to live in contaminated environments, and how to protect your children from its lethal effects.

Let us try to formulate the few rules that will help us to raise our children in good health - as well as ourselves.

There is a fact we cannot deny: there has indeed been a disaster at the Chernobyl nuclear power plant, having a tremendous impact on our way of life, with similar consequences as the disaster in Fukushima nuclear plant will have on the Japanese. It is a fact we cannot ignore. But there is another undeniable fact: to a large extent, we are able to limit the effects of radiation on human health. As we have seen, what is required to protect ourselves against this radioactivity is neither expensive nor dependent on decisions and directives from the government. We must understand that we have only ourselves to rely on. We must get rid of the unhappy victim role and stop waiting for an "uncle from America" who will come to solve all our problems. Certainly charitable organizations worldwide give invaluable assistance to Belarusian children, but the basis still depends on ourselves:

1. Everything in our surroundings and the people themselves must undergo radiological control. First and foremost, you have to control contamination in foods. You need to take every given

opportunity to control the content of radionuclides in milk, mushrooms, berries, and other products you drink and eat.

2. Foodstuffs, which contain radionuclides that exceed the limits, are unsuitable for consumption. Do not eat them!

3. You must remove mushrooms and wild game from the children's menu. Radionuclides they ingest by eating these products will harm children much more than any benefits they might have from such foods.

4. Know that proper (culinary and technical) preparation of these foods may lower their radiation content significantly. This of course requires time, but do not debate this: it's for your own good and for the good of your children. You'll get to spend more time in the kitchen, but on the other hand, God willing, you will live longer.

5. If your vegetable garden is located in a contaminated area, follow the methods for soil improvement and fertilization that we recommend here for the vegetable garden, if it is located in a contaminated area. They are not complicated and are very effective.

6. Every citizen in the contaminated zone of Chernobyl must have a mandatory measurement of accumulation of radionuclides in the whole body at least twice a year. If experts from the Belrad Institute come to your place, do not let this opportunity pass to monitor your and your children's contamination. Follow the recommendations you will receive in connection with the results.

7. Consult with physicians in your region to know what products you can use to reduce the amount of radionuclides in the body.

8. If your child has been given pectin products at school, ensure that they are taken regularly. Explain to the children that it is absolutely necessary that they take pectin products regularly, for them to grow well, to stay healthy and to turn into strong adults able to form a family and give you healthy grandchildren.

We often hear it being said around us: "I'm not going to be tested. The less you know, the better you sleep ... ". It is possible that you sleep better but unfortunately you risk not sleeping very long... Knowing is a prerequisite for protecting yourself. If you are informed, if you know the risk, if you know what to do, you may be able to prevent a number of unfortunate consequences.

The usual statement, that the radioactivity disappeared a long time ago, and that one should not think about it, is unfortunately false. The radiation is still present, it's going to be here a long, long time and we must not underestimate it.

In contaminated areas, we often hear a claim that strong alcohol (vodka) eliminates radioactivity. Alcohol eliminates small gray brain cells, affecting the liver and heart. Everyone knows that excessive alcohol consumption is unhealthy. If you then add the effects of radioactivity, you get a nice cocktail! Why should one voluntarily rush towards the grave?

We are often asked if the children gain any advantage from the holidays they spend in Belarusian sanatoria or abroad. No doubt. Belrad often works in sanatoria and preventive institutions. The fact that children get "clean" food, that children's health is being monitored, that they may follow the most modern cures can only do them good. We have observed that a stay in the sanatorium "Silversprings" in Svetlogorsk district not only makes it possible to lower children's radioactive contamination, but also leads to a decline in other disorders. At the same time the children get some useful knowledge about ecology. The same goes for other preventive establishments in Belarus – the children's sanatorium in Otrochitski Gorodok or health centres Jdanovitchi and Ozerny.

A stay abroad is also beneficial because children experience an uncontaminated, "clean" environment, they eat clean food and breathe clean air. But we need to be very attentive in order to avoid regrettable abuse: we have reported several cases in which parents had fed the children with contaminated products with the only intent, to get them sent to a stay abroad. What an absolutely incredible callousness! Who can rescue a child if it accumulates radionuclides not only because of its environment, but also because of its parents' misdeeds!

CONCLUSION – EPILOGUE

This text is originally intended for families and teachers of Belarusian schools and ends with a fervent appeal to remain united and organized in the face of the endless threat of radioactive fallout that covers more than a quarter of the country. This fallout is spread over larger and larger areas, through runoff, wind and fire. While the radioactivity decreases by a factor of 2 every thirty years, the overall situation becomes more and more complex.

This book emphasizes the indispensable role an organization like the Belrad Institute plays in maintaining a unique base of knowledge and guaranteeing that it will be passed on to new generations. Belrad is the hub for independent knowledge of the country, - independent of any political or economic project, not subject to any government's will to put Chernobyl to an end. Independence comes hand in hand with a lack of funds. Because the land is poor, made even poorer by radioactive pollution, restrictions on agricultural activities and the reluctance of possible investors, the populations in the poorest regions are not able to finance their own radiation protection. The book acknowledges the German, English, Austrian and Irish organizations that helped to save the institute at the beginning of the 1990s.

The organization Children of Chernobyl Belarus has created a relationship with their Belarusian partners based on equality: it's a win-win situation, by no way "humanitarian aid", because we need to learn from the research on the real consequences such a nuclear accident has on environmental and public health. Cooperation with Belrad takes place through formal economic agreements with time frames that cover one or more years of radiation protection campaigns for many thousands of compromised children in defined areas, listing up the villages to monitor. In return Belrad submits monthly activity reports, and supplies an uninterrupted database of records as collected in the "Atlas of radiation-contamination in the general population." More than 430,000 measurements have been classified and represent unparalleled scientific background material. Contributions to Belrad, or those to the Laboratory of Genetic Safety, follow the same financing: payment at request or pro forma invoice.

Let us imagine that a serious accident takes place in Western Europe and that our country will be affected, as was the case in Belarus, Ukraine and South Western Russia. Let us imagine that the historical miracle a Belrad Institute represents and the repeated small miracles that secure the funds for the institute to stay afloat and to undertake it's work - had NOT occurred, or that our programs had ceased. This would mean that there was only one single voice present - that of the official national and international authorities on health and radiation safety: they proclaim that Chernobyl = 50 dead and several thousand cases of thyroid cancer - "curable or preventable". Beyond that, people's complaints have nothing to do with radiation but are first and foremost due to the <u>fear</u> of radiation: radiation phobia (a disease invented there and then at the end of 1988 to give a reason for the explosion in the number of somatic diseases among residents of the contaminated areas; the notion of radiation phobia is of course rejected by those who disapprove the official reports). The official disinformation would be spread all over the world, without any contradiction at all.

Our country would then experience the same health tragedy that has hit the three Soviet republics since the late 80's. And our authorities would repeat what the World Health Organization and the Japanese administration have done after Fukushima: they would psychologise in one swoop all illnesses that might arise - except cancer of the thyroid, the only disease that they admit to be caused by radiation...

Meanwhile, scientific work and on-site observations of the population affected by Chernobyl show that **the only radiation exposure that is completely harmless - is zero radiation.** Experience shows that zero radiation is a level that it is not possible to achieve. Experience also shows that the motivation to take precaution is highly fragile over years and decades. The general breakdown of public health, especially of the young, provokes fatalism and a deep sense of powerlessness. The funds Belrad disposes of only enables them to deal with a small percentage of the problem - and this in a rather superficial way, carrying out visits only twice a year where the need is for four or eight times! In spite of great efforts to prevent damage, and all the information and training given, each monitoring-campaign reminds us of that it is virtually impossible for parents and children to constantly avoid consuming contaminated food.

It is easy to believe that Japan is better equipped and prepared to deal with the consequences of Fukushima than the Soviet Union in 1986. That is completely wrong. The Soviet Union was preparing for nuclear war, threatened by (U.S.) President Reagan. At that time it was defined and read aloud what procedures should be followed in answer to the radiation levels expected on the battlefield. Therefore the Chernobyl war became a blitz war that ended with the construction of the concrete "containment" at the beginning of fall 1986. But this was just one stroke. The enemy had occupied extensive areas far from the battlefields around the power plant.

It is also easy to believe that Japan through its wealth is set in a more favourable position to tackle the second phase, which still paralyzes the contaminated regions of the former Soviet Russia. Also this is a mistake: a rich country, but at the same time also a quite small one, means housing prices are out of reach. The relocation of evacuees from Chernobyl - more than 250 000 in all, has obviously cost the country less than it would cost Japan to do so. Thinking of Japan as more favourable equipped is above all erroneous because the "*Atomic and Radiation Lobby*" has taken the leadership in Japan - with a communication strategy perfected by lessons from Chernobyl.

Finally, we can say that the USSR in the time of Glasnost and Perestroika undoubtedly gave greater freedom to a variety of initiatives than a Japanese democracy constrained by major political and industrial pressure groups: an ideal terrain for the International Atomic Energy Agency IAEA to operate freely. It is the IAEA who has been entrusted with the responsibility to manage the radioactive crisis in the country! (According to their statutes, the IAEA is conceived to spread nuclear power for peaceful means...) Until now, there is no sign of a Japanese Nesterenko but let us not despair, the Japanese society is fermenting.

Arriving at the end of this publication, let us try an exhausting thought exercise: let's apply what this little book has taught us, to a British - or European context. The laws of physics do not care about borders, nationalities or technological nuances. Same cause = same effect! There's NO clean nuclear technology, either civilian or military (as opposed to a myth created in 1962, the date of the first French nuclear bomb testing, the European/ French bomb is as dirty, if not worse - because more powerful, than an Iranian bomb would be.) The consequences of a radiation accident would have the same impact, and the ensuing restraints would be the same. Our government would repeat the same errors as their Japanese counterparts have shown by many examples, by believing in that decontaminating by flushing buildings or by scraping away the superficial surface of some parcels of land here and there! By all means, do not evacuate, do not undertake the only measure that would provide effective protection, but would be the most expensive in the short term.

There would not be any British/ European Nesterenko among us, for the simple reason that none of the bosses of the "atomic club", neither after Chernobyl nor after Fukushima, have switched sides to proclaim:

It's enough! Stop!

Yves Lenoir March 2012,
chair of "Enfants de Chernobyl", France

SOME SCIENTIFIC REFERENCES OF THE BELRAD-INSTITUTE

V.B.Nesterenko, L.V.Bordak, V.B.Nesterenko, Institute of Radiation Protection BELRAD, *Nutritional Supplements based on pectin for radiation protection of the Belarusian population, the medical consequences of the Chernobyl catastrophe: results of 15 in Medical Consequences of the Chernobyl Disaster: Results of 15 Years of Research*, 3 International Conference, 4-8 June 2001 Kiev, Ukraine, abstracts published in "Journal international de medicine radiologique", Edition spéciale Vol.3, Nr 1-2, 2001,
www.enfants-tchernobyl-belarus.org/doku.php?id=base_documentaire:articles-2001:etb-11

V.B.Nesterenko, A.N.Devoino, I.E.Nesterenko, V.V.Golub, A.V.Vinnikov, A.A.Mukhlaev, Institute of Radiation Protection BELRAD, *Direct measurements of accumulation levels of radioactive cesium in foodstuffs and the organism of the Belarusian population in areas contaminated by Chernobyl, in Medical Consequences of the Chernobyl Disaster: Results of 15 Years of Research*, 3. International Conference, 4-8 June 2001, Kiev, Ukraina, abstract published in "Journal international de medicine radiologique", Edition spéciale Vol.3, Nr 1-2, 2001.

Y.I.Bandazhevsky V.B.Nesterenko, stråleverninstituttet BELRAD, *Measurements of Cs137 and public health, in Medical Consequences of the Chernobyl Disaster: Results of 15 Years of Research*, 3. International Conference, 4-8 June 2001, Kiev, Ukraina, abstract published in "Journal international de medicine radiologique", Edition spéciale Vol.3, Nr 1-2, 2001.

V.B.Nesterenko, A.N.Devoyno, A.A.Mukhlayev, I.E.Nesterenko, *State and Dynamics of the Radiation Contamination of Foodstuffs for Children in the Chernobyl Zone of Belarus According to the Data from Local Radi-*

ation Control Centres, International Journal of Radiation Medicine 2004, 6(1-4): 122-129, *www.physiciansofchernobyl.org.ua/magazine/PDFS/si6_2004/6_18.pdf*

V.B.Nesterenko, A.V.Nesterenko, I.V.Babenko, T.V.Yerkovich, I.V.Babenko, *Reducing the 137Cs-load in the organism of "Chernobyl" children with apple pectin,* SWISS MED WKLY 2004;134:24-27. *www.smw.ch*

G.S.Bandazhevskaya, V.B.Nesterenko, V.I.Babenko, I.V.Babenko, T.V.Yerkovich, Y.I.Bandazhevsky; Institute of Radiation Safety BELRAD, Minsk, republic of Belarus, *Relationship between cesium (137Cs) load, cardiovascular symptoms, and source of food in "Chernobyl" children – preliminary observations after intake of oral apple pectin,* SWISS MED WKLY 2004; 134:725-729. *www.smw.ch*

V.B.Nesterenko, *Radiological monitoring of population and food intake in the Chernobyl region of Belarus,* in collaboration with A.Devoïno, V.I.Babenko, I.Nesterenko, A.V.Nesterenko, A.Mukhlaev, T.Erkovitch, I.Babenko, A.Potapoiv, O.Nesterenko, M.Kozyremko, M.Khromov, V.Derugo, Informajonsbulletin nr. 28, BELRAD, Minsk, 2005

Dossier ATLAS, utdrag, BELRAD,

www.enfants-tchernobyl-belarus.org/doku.php?id=base_documentaire:articles-2001:etb-65

www.tredition.de

AFTER THE NUCLEAR ACCIDENT - HOW TO PROTECT AGAINST RADIATION – A PRACTICAL GUIDE

Author: **Vladimir Babenko**

Translated and adapted from the French version (*Après l'accident atomique*) to English by Susanne Urban

© 2013 Susanne Urban

First issue English version: February 2014

Coverdesign, illustration: mariourban.com

Fonts: **Futura**
Mignon Pro 11/12, 9
Cover paperback, matt
Papirtype: chamois

Forlag: tredition GmbH, Hamburg

Paperback ISBN: 978-3-8495-7555-7

Printed in Germany

Bibliographic information published by Deutsche Nationalbibliothek:
The German National Library shows this publication in the Deutsche National Bibliography; detailed bibliographic data are available on the internet at *http://dnb.d-nb.de*.